In Between the Lines

Akanksha Sharma

BookLeaf Publishing

India | USA | UK

Presentation by *BookLeaf Publishing*

Web: www.bookleafpub.com

E-mail: info@bookleafpub.com

ISBN: 9789358731491

First edition 2023

DEDICATION

I dedicate my first book to the Union of Hope and Honesty; perpetual faith and ceaseless love.

And every reader who finds their feelings written between the lines of any stanza in this book.

ACKNOWLEDGEMENT

A lot goes into making a lady a poetess; pain, people, and words. In my story it was all three of them; the pain and pins that pierced my heart and inked a permanent tattoo of poetry on it, the people who left or never left my side in this journey called life, and the words that I play with; all of these made me a poetess that I am grateful and indebted to the Lord for.

I want to address the publishers at BookLeaf to give me this support and opportunity to bring my words to valued readers. I can't go without thanking my confidants for reading my poems when the world was asleep, you own a big lump of this milestone.

PREFACE

Dear Reader,

You probably don't know me personally, but even if you do, nobody really knows anyone deep enough to understand the person that exists beneath the multiple layers and facade that they put on every day before facing the world. The poems that you are about to read in the coming pages are all very close to my heart, they are little snippets from incidents of my life that made my muse take the front seat in my head and drove me into the madness of being a poetess. Not everything that I write is my first-hand experience but reading the room has always been my secret talent. All that I saw and felt somewhere got translated into poetry and ended up here in your hands.

This is my first book, I am nervous, scared, elated, vulnerable, and ecstatic all at once. It is definitely surreal to feel so many things at the same time but I do not fear sharing this with you.

I am bringing this compilation to you with honesty and hope; in the process of writing I incidentally immortalized these emotions, and today you are embarking on this journey with me to read those emotions and feel them as raw as I did when I wrote them.

I can't say I am not skeptical, but I believe in the power of words and that assures me that this book "In Between the Lines" will tickle a place in your heart that was still untouched.

Welcome to the heart-to-heart conversation in the form of poetry, I invite you to read the works of my muse.

Her

When giving up was easy,
She stood her ground to fight
Bullet holes hollowed her chest,
Backstabbed with multiple knives.
Yet in her I saw a mighty knight

Tears clouding her sight,
She looked me in the eye.
A faint smile embraced her cheek,
"Fight" her lips mumbled in agony
Was I going to see a fighter die?

I closed my eyes in denial,
Tears drowned her face, it was a goodbye...
Quivering she placed her palm on mine
Veiled, she united in my reflection
That day the mirror heard my loudest cry.

Prophecy

She pulled hard on the strings of her destiny,
To dissolve the unfair prophecy
To untangle the wires of her luck

She fought misery with smiles, and despair with
hope
She cures people with her poetry, and pain with
what she wrote
Brewing words in an emotional elixir, bringing
back lives and luck.

Her muse was the glistening agony behind her
eyes,
She gathers all the sadness of the world, but
never cries...
And with all that pain, sorrow, and hurt she
writes

She wrote about you, about all the things you
hide
Even how you wished she died
You wished her pain but she returned the favour
in kind.

But she's a descendant of an Amazon
Break her? Oh you cannot.
She will rise back stronger each time she falls.

Today the serendipitous lioness roared,
Her words mightier than the world's strongest
sword.
And she declared the unfair prophecy dissolved.

You Never Loved Her

Of all the things she loves,
You're her favourite heart.
In broken pieces of your soul
All she sees is love and art.

Of all the stories she brews,
You're her favourite character.
In your faux and faults
All she sees is smiles and laughter.

Of all the letters she has compiled,
None made their way to you
In your wait, she ceased to exist
All she ever desired was a rendezvous

Of all the things she mentioned loving,
Momentarily your name slips her mouth
In your awe, she forgot naming herself
Her love was pure, but unfair and uncouth.

Of all she was, she was yours to love
Time passed and went by in a blur
She was always present for you
Yet you never loved her.

Moon and Me

Last night I talked with the moon...
She cried to me about her love, Sun
And I cried to her about you
We sobbed all night, in the distance...
To drench the morning in dew

As the night grew dark and deep
She says, her glimmer is all love...
I said my smile is about love too
We talked a lot, but fell still and silent...
She missed the sun, while I missed you

Her tears drained into the sea...
Mine could just wet my pillow and sheets
It was soon going to be dawn..
Her shimmer returned, she will meet the sun
But I didn't smile, because you're still away and
gone.

A Mile with Hope

Hope is absurd

She met my gaze and stole my heart
In her eyes, I saw promises
She made me wait

She held my hand but broke my heart
On her lips were lies and longing
She made me vulnerable

But hope embraced me at last
In her arms, I was unharmed
She made me unbreakable

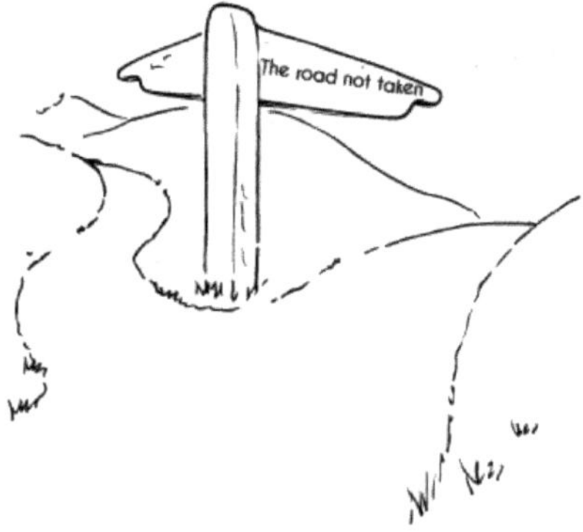

Alone

Alone, betrayed and broken
In a war with ourselves
When the world sat unaware
We fought our despair

Never give up,
We learnt Silently fighting the suffering
When winning over the catastrophe
Was the only hope

Picked up our pieces
Some pierced and hurt
We hunched they'll heal
And wore the "alright" veil

With the strongest will
A firm support and a little push
We fought hardships in the past
It was only our hope at last

Life threw sour lemons
Taking it with a smile
Accepting the fate
We made sweet lemonade

All this while we had faith
Better things will always come
And out of everything we will elope
After all the world lives on hope.

Night

We've all complained about the dark,
We're all praises for the light...
But when we were trudging uphill
When we were tired and dried
My friend, we all were kept safe
We had a shield, this unlit night.

We've all feared the dungeons of the dark.
We never questioned the locks of the light...
But when we were falling face first,
When we needed a space to hide
We cried and screamed in her arms
We were comforted, by this somber night

Still not Lost

I am lost in an abyss
In the tranquility of my thoughts
World is Purple
And my eyes are red
Heart long gone, probably dead

Why is it so irrefutable?
Why is my heart so full?
All I need is something...
Or someone to call mine, my abditory
And their heart my territory

I want to hide and never confide
From the cruel kith and kin alike
World Scares my soul
I can no more put up a fight
I want to hide, from everyone's sight.

I wear Black to dissolve
I stand out instead.
Looking down I walk...
To avoid every gaze I crossed
But to them, I am still not lost

Poetry

Her heart's at war with her mind,
A thousand thoughts pierce her heart,
It's dying an untimely death
And the mind has taken over with stealth

She's locked in dungeons of her past,
Her mind wouldn't stop until the final kill
Fate has put her heart to the test,
To come out alive of her mind's tempest

It's time to resurrect the dead
To revive her heart and rekindle love
She's a warrior, not a damsel in distress
She bleeds ink, writing with no regrets

One thought at a time, in one inbreathe
She pulls out the arrows one by one...
And let her heart bleed and greave
Her mind stops, and all she does is feel

Words pour out of the rim of her eyes
Sliding down the curves of her cheeks
She scribbles and writes hopelessly...
And with all that pain cries in poetry.

Nightingale

Glittering water, peaceful ripples
Above the night sky twinkles
Humming a sweet melody
Sitting by the lake she crafts poetry
Weaving emotions between the lines
Her words drip nectar.

Honey flows down her pen
Dropping a veil on her feign
Hiding behind a disguise
She writes till sunrise
As the sun touches the ground, she leaves
Eloping without her unfinished letter

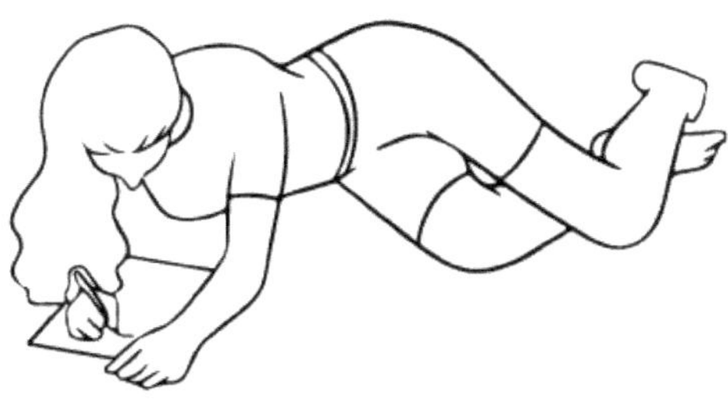

To the Moon and Back

Millennials ago this story began,
When Distance still held us apart.
It was with your first smile.
I was ready to cross this mile.

Your gaze when falls on me.
It makes me glitter in your light
With all that reflecting in my waters...
Every passerby's heart flatters.

My heartbeats quicken..
To reach you there I try..
Nowhere I let my efforts halt.
Repeatedly my waves somersault.

As the morning goes down,
And the stars begin to show...
I wait for you from where I lie..
Gazing for your presence up in the sky.

Shimmering beneath your beauty,
Proudly the splashes sing,
Making melody out of shells,
Onset of romance propels.

When slowly the night darkens,
I hear your message to me,
When the crickets stridulate
My water rises and I acidulate.

Under the stary lit roof,
Buds of our love blossoms.
Initiating another rendezvous,
Giving us a sense of deja vu.

But now it's time to return,
Our little date has to end.
With a promise to meet again,
The ritual of goodbyes began.

The silhouette of you disappears..
And the sunrays creep up,
Staining the horizon red.
Again putting my thoughts to bed.

Going back from the rocks..
Dew drops tell me you wept.
Sadly even I left the shore..
Leaving shells and conches as hints ashore.

Though it ends here today,
I'll love you till the moon and back.
We may be made to part,
But only in distance love never in heart.

Meant to be

I promised my heart,
To never fall in love again...
But it whispered to me your name

It knew before me,
That to you it's destined to belong
And it'll be worth it even after so long

I am all yours only yours...
In our own kind of forever and beyond
We will never break this promise bond

You fell first but I fell harder...
But your arms cushioned my fall
And I realized love is not painful at all

In you I found my muse,
In love you're all I see
After all my love we were always meant to be

Chin Up Princess

Silent stares, loud judgements
Calculating eyes and blabbering mouths.
Eyeing the fit of your shirt.
Measuring the length of your skirt,

Determined to make nasty remarks,
They're everywhere.
To pull you down when you rise,
They befriend you with their disguise.

In you my dear friend
With unapologetic curtness,
Unnecessary flaws they'll find.
But this is something you shouldn't mind.

Behind a keyboard they might hide.
Trolling you on social media is their delight.
Darling you're free to fight
But pay no heed and slap them tight.

Power up your game.
Keep working towards your goals.
Change your lefts into your rights.
Don't you shiver, achieve those heights.

Promise yourself,
You'll stand against them.
There will be no " if, but, can't, and or"
Because baby that's not what you're made for.

Enrich yourself daily.
Heal, grow and prosper.
You'll be what you want to be.
No more be a 'tormented she'

Trust your dreams, chase your aims.
Don't let them decide it for you.
Cook, design, dance, shoot or climb walls.
But chin up princess or the crown falls.

Playdate

Tears, sweat, blood, and ink,
Blended together into it.
Some laughed, some praised…
But was forgotten in a wink.

Thousands of midnights,
She spent awake.
Scribbling in her notebook,
Staring at the shimmering lake.

A drop slipped down her eye,
She wiped it off.
Turned the lampshade on..
And stole the stars from the night sky.

It was now a routine,
Poetry was her playmate...
Together with words they played,
Enjoying their little, inked date.

Applause and praises came by...
Bestsellers one after the other...
Everyone admired the writings
But none saw the writer cry!

Faith

I was tied, trapped, and lost
In the dungeons of my own desires
Where the dark meets no light
I was tired, pained of putting up a fight

Attraction clutched my feet, hunger held my
wrists
Want of power turned me blue with injuries
Dark of my desires, drowned my every limb
And to break free, I remembered him

With every syllable of his name,
A wound healed, and a tie broke...
With every blow thrown at my way...
All my pains and sins washed away.

In his name I found love, peace, and salvation
In him I found my heart, I bowed down on his
feet,
He is my saviour, I surrendered to my God...
And I found my purpose in reward

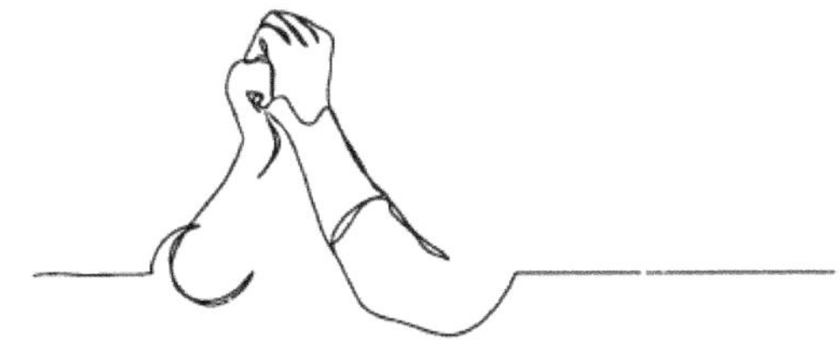

You and Me

We've been through storms,
The world knows nothing about.
Behind the veils and walls,
We're all raw and broken.

We've been called a failure,
The world is full of remorse.
Behind the facade of success,
We're all wandering and lost.

We've been pretending throughout,
The world celebrates it.
Behind the scenes of this play.
We're all same, both you and me.

Scribbles

Held that pen again today...
With a firm grip of fingers.
And a head hung low...
As the ink was adamant not to flow.

All that I could hear was...
'Poetry is a waste of time'
Replaying this in my brain..
I lost all my words dime by dime.

Lamp by my bed dimmed...
Mirroring my words and thoughts.
My reddened eyes scanned, The gibberish stanza
I wrote...
Until I knew what loss of words costs.

There went another page..
Crumpled onto the floor...
startled by my inability I sighed..
One last time, I again lied.

Tried the thousandth time,
Efforts still in vain.
I flushed down my grumpy scribbles
And watched it go down the drain

Museum Wall

Hearts are museums, of the life we lived
And the esteem and love we once adored
It holds onto memories of all we endured

Empty canvases, and spotless pages
Bare white walls devoid of any art
Nothing ever touched me, to paint it on my heart

But my heart wouldn't remain barren
Or vacant museum of empty canvases
So I started painting it with my catharsis

Words are now etched on the walls of my heart
I hold them as dear as the big red scar
That I got when I let love paint it bizarre

World as I See It

Boundless and infinite, my world ends nowhere
It sways merrily on life's melody...
At one time so hopeful, but another moment in
despair
Alike a soulful and timeless parody...

Not cruel, it is not even kind
It is as you perceive it, by heart and mind
Brewing lies and truth at the same time
My world is as I am, sweet always somedays lime

At the edge of time, my world hangs upside down,
Supported by the string of lingering hope.
I believe in my power, I'll not let it drown
For my love binds the strings of this rope.

Friends and foes, my world treats all alike
It doesn't hate nor it does like
Your action is what the world will return
It comes back for a repay, turn by turn.

Ecstasy

I knew roses to be red
And the skies to be blue...
But today they changed their hue.

Nothing is in place, everything seems alien
This is not haunting me
As it used to be

It is inviting me to its beautiful embrace
To it is capturing and alluring spell
The kind even the strongest wizards can't repel

Is this happening only to me?
Am I drowning in faith and trust
My Choices no longer seem just

Love and poetry have taken over me
It makes my vision blurry and eyes glassy
I discovered my own Ecstasy

Death of Poetry

Another paper crumpled
Off the window, it goes.
Twenty scratches later...
Finally, the ink flows.

My pen was stuck, ink absent
And to write I try
Crumbling at it again
I let out a wailing sigh...

All my words lie unuttered,
Rusted like an edgeless sword
And the heart lies overwhelmed
With the "I can't do it award"

Always when I wanted to pull the trigger
I picked up a pen instead
And now with the muse gone
I already feel dead.

Overthinking?

I wonder how you will remember me…
When I'll no longer speak or breathe
Will you hold me close and weep?

I wonder if you will know my strength when I'm
gone
When you will find that note of what I went
through
Or will you still blame me for being weak?

I wonder, how many me it will take
For the world to finally be kind and compassionate
Or will it always return to the chaos and rat race?

Do I wonder too much?
For the things that never happened, nor will ever
be…
And the world was right in not using their thoughts
as much as me

Heart's in a Cage

When the world was loyal, and life was being
made
Hearts were on the loose, free, and unconfined.
Humans wore them on their sleeves.
Hate didn't exist and love was always blind.

When the hearts met their mate,
Their beats hummed a twin melody,
And their strings intertwined…
It could stretch far and beyond, and we called it
'destiny'

Nothing else mattered, only hearts fell in love
But then came to an apocalypse called 'lust'
Soulmates were hard to find, love lost its
meaning
Wrong strings intertwined and birthed pain and
mistrust

Hearts couldn't pass the test of time,
They were punished to grieve till the end of age
The strings of destiny disappeared, and no hearts
are on the loose
They are now held captured in the rib cage.

Persephone's Choice

She is an angel, but the devil sits on her left
Her heart is made of silver, gold runs in her veins
Her smile shines, but pitch dark are her brains

She is the spring, a blooming Florette
But get on her wrongs, and you will regret
Her eyes can light up your pyre and burn you in
hell.

She was held captive against her will…
Oppressed and dragged to the abode of the dead
But she emerged as their queen instead.

She had to choose, to be a modest nymph
Or to take a chance and jump off a cliff
She took a chance and caused a change

Today she is both, a part creation and another
death
She wins with love and ruins with a felony
And she chose to become Persephone.

Storyteller

I will steal you from your inhibitions, I promise
you the land of stars.
If only you promise me, not to hide your
unhealed scars.
I will be your voice, it will be your tears but my
eyes.
I will be your words, but I will tell your tale.
Let it be known to the world, I will not let you
fail.

Drop down the facade, and let the layers of
opinions fall
Wake up! Stand up against your vices, I know
you'll stand tall.
All that has been done, needs to be dusted off
We can start fresh and let the bygones be
bygones
Shall we begin with crushing your sky-high
isolation walls?

Confide in me, your deepest desires and darkest
secret
About your lost smile, and what piques your
interest
I will believe in you, even when you cannot

You're not alone, and it is not just your battle to
fight
I'll be there by your side in this tunnel until we
see white light.

Remember, how the villain is a hero when his
story is being told
All his intentions are justified and no longer
uncouth and cold
We are all characters, playing our broken and
flawed parts
Let me be your listener or send me your
unposted letter
And I promise you to be your supporter, your
storyteller

My Lookalike

Darkness embraced me in a hug when the light
was unkind,
Stabs and insults kept me awake until my ears
bled
But she lulled me to sleep when I cried.

She was my age, we looked almost alike
But she was all guts and bravery
And here I am a poor sight

She picked the fights and I received the blows
While she was valiant, I was the feeble kind
When she sneered, I'd still pick sorrows

World denied her existence, but I was a living
testimony
It was my tears that flowed through her eyes
And she held me in her arms when I was lonely

She could be a little feisty at times
So I push her back in my head, where she
belongs
But, when I cry she talks to me like yestertimes

Her voice rang in my ears, "Fight" she said
I stood my ground for the first time
And I realized, She was not just a voice in my
head.

In her somber, I found my inner light
She braved the darkness so I could shine
And even today, to meet her, I never sleep in the
night

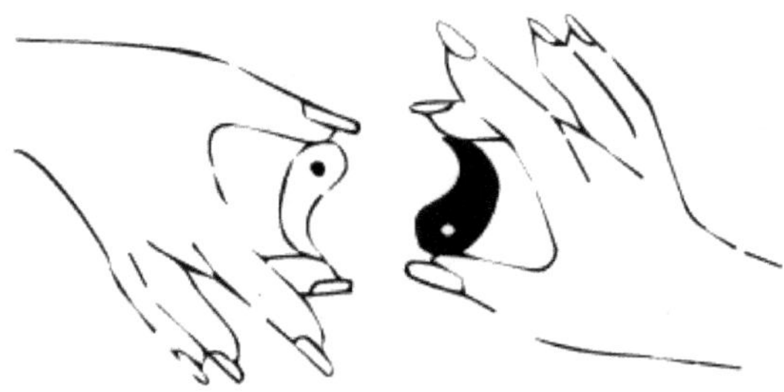

Apology

Apologise, you scream at me.
But why should I?
When, you started the hurting spree

You were here to protect
And yet chose to break me instead
How do I trust you, with all that you left wrecked?

You hurt me with all that you could
All I did was slap back with my words
Then why am I left misunderstood?

I apologised, for the sake of respect
You turned around the narrative
It is true, the innocent ones always repent

You set me on fire, can't you see?
With all that you said, I am hurt beyond repair. The
one asking for an apology should have been me.

I never got my revenge and you will be gone
before me...
But the scars you gave me will immortalize
And remind me, of the void of an apology.

Goodbye!

The sky wept on your departure,
But not as much as my heart...
How could you leave this world,
Bereaving your little one falling apart?

I crave your words, even if it is a scolding.
I miss your embrace, I never had that enough
If only you could return once, and hug me tight
Your child yearns for your love.

Today, as I kneel beside your gray bed,
Wishing for your return in my prayer
A thousand pins pierce my seething heart
I cry to God, ask him why is he so unfair.

All the words that died on my feeble lips
I can feel them flowing out of the corner of my
eye
Wishing if only I had said "I love you" often
If only I could kiss you my final Good Bye!!

1871

The world is a garden, and I am just another
flower.

But the one that refuses to wither and die
I will prick those who would pluck me for my
beauty
But I will blossom, for those with an obliged
eye.

Not the one you'd want to smell, nor the easiest
to find
I'll be the wildflower withstanding the test of
time
I am just another flower, with beauty and thorns
combined.

_the wildflower